Mrs. Hamilton -
Happy EASter
and God's Blessings
Love,
Janie
H/2010

Children of a
Rhythmless World

and other poems

Janice Beaty Springs

authorHOUSE®

AuthorHouse™
1663 Liberty Drive, Suite 200
Bloomington, IN 47403
www.authorhouse.com
Phone: 1-800-839-8640

This book is a work of fiction. People, places, events, and situations are the product of the author's imagination. Any resemblance to actual persons, living or dead, or historical events, is purely coincidental.

First published by AuthorHouse   12/15/2008

ISBN: 978-1-4389-2419-9 (sc)

Printed in the United States of America
Bloomington, Indiana

This book is printed on acid-free paper.

This book is dedicated to
MY DAUGHTER, TYRA LYNETTE THOMPSON
and all the beautiful
delicate flowers that
continue to blossom

Table of Contents

Acknowledgements

First, and foremost, I thank The Creator, the infinite and eternal source of my strength. I thank my mother, Dora Patton Beaty – who introduced me to my faith. I thank all of my siblings who spawned in me an ability to love selflessly, and the many people with whom I have crossed paths and benefited from their words of wisdom, inspiration and encouragement.

"Purpose is not about being liked by other people, being famous, or becoming rich. It is about knowing who you are and putting that knowledge to use in a meaningful way."

-- Iyanla Vanzant, <u>The Value in the Valley</u>

Beginnings

Let's Pretend

i want to pretend
we are back then
when it didn't matter
if you had a nickel
or if i had a dime
or if your hair
was longer than mine
or if i called you fat
or if you stepped on a crack
and broke your mamma's back
as the fireflies in our jars
shone brighter than the stars
or if dew-moistened bare toes
caused drippy runny nose.

i want to pretend
we are back then
i want to sit
on the porch with you
share a bag of chips
savor salt-covered fingertips
i want to drink a bottle of coke
fall out laughing over a silly joke
eat some squirrel nuts or BB bats

ignore repercussions of midsection fat
watch fireworks on a cool fall night
take pleasure in the booming delight
wrapped in warmth that mom's quilt brings
hand-made with love from old jeans and things
let's pretend
we are back then.

Just My Mom and Me

When I was two or three
Often you could find me

Clinging to her skirt with thumb in my mouth
Just my mom and me

My thumb was my soothing calm
The kitchen always nice and warm

Mom washing off juicy tomatoes
Or, for candied yams, slicing sweet potatoes

Mom often prayed during those times
Privy to her prayers, I'd listen to each line

I'd listen as she'd call out His name
Her voice sometimes filled with pain

She sometimes cried as she prayed
Her words in my little heart stayed

She would worriedly cry out her fears
Food, clothing, all the bills
He'd always answered her prayers before

So she'd seek Him out just once more

Feeling her distress, anguish and pain
I too would call out His holy name

Please answer my mommy's prayers
Her pain at my little heart tears

A day or two would go by
And once again, I'd hear her cry

Yet this time there was joy and no pain
As she'd passionately call out His name

Once again He'd answered her prayers
Faithfully, yes, He truly cares

And now in times of joy and pain
I too call out His holy name

And, as I am so reverently aware
He always answers my every prayer

Clinging to her skirt with thumb in my mouth
Just my mom and me

A Queen's Masterpiece

Determination - when a lone mother of seven
Refuses to allow societal dictates to prophetize
her outcome
I see her alone
Feeding, clothing and comforting
Her babies
Working late-night hours in the stench
Of dust-filled tobacco quarters
Returning home covered in that same dust

I see her shaking this dust from headscarves
Whose faded colors once flaunted bright prints
Designed to be worn in pretty places
Yet, this determined Queen
Had no time for pretty places

I see her, pushed by a dogged determination
Cleansing homes of the privileged
Without pausing in between
For a restful respite

I see a sponge enveloped
In a smooth brown hand
Running over expensive porcelain

Removing all traces of grime
Bringing back luminous sheen to be
Enjoyed by others
This Queen sees only her babies' faces
Reflected in mirrored sheens she creates

Then, as time passes, I see this Queen again
A face non-reflective of hard work
Or worried, sleepless nights
After years of fate's testing hand,
There is no trace of bitterness or resentment,
No hint of malevolence, or spite

A face that shows no signs
Of having labored in the tobacco-dust-filled
quarters
I see smooth brown hands
That lack evidence of years of scrubbing
Other's expensive porcelain

I see a Queen whose face is as
Rich and smooth as the same
Expensive porcelain she once cleansed
I see a soft smile reflecting pride,
Genuineness, love, joy and laughter, peace…
I see an artist whose stance replicates

The pride of having just completed a
masterpiece

This Queen's masterpiece
Her babies - seven
A painting reflecting radiant colors of
Principles, wisdom, caring, perseverance,
patience, determination, love...
A work well done by a beautiful determined
Queen!

The World Today

Children of a Rhythmless World

The world is losing it rhythm
As doves crash into translucent prisms
Of man-made cold steel towers
And the silence of a rhythmless world
Is broken by laughter of boys and girls
True joy and glee they negate
And seek humor in the dove's sad fate
Unaware of the hollow black void
Where their own faces used to be.

The world is losing its rhythm
As mothers drive their faceless children
Into depths of translucent lakes
And again the silence of a rhythmless world
Is broken by screams of boys and girls
Their sorrow and pain so innate
They find comfort in their own dire fate
Unaware of the hollow black void
Where their own "souls" used to be.

Soon Come

She's quivering!
Can't you feel it?
Excitement and anticipation
Pores dripping with perspiration
Spills over membrane beaches
Desperate finger of tsunami reaches

She's quivering!
Can't you feel it?
Menopausal clock's alarm
Hot flashes cause global warm
Glowing lava seeps from erupting pores
Covering miles and miles of thirsty seashores

She's quivering!
Can't you feel it?
Anticipating the coming of her King
Shaking and shivering throughout her being
Surrounding air does twist and twirl
Hurricanes and tornadoes frenziedly swirl

She's quivering!
Can't you feel it?
Her excitement she can hardly contain

Relief from centuries of abuse and pain
For she knows that time's nearly done
Her Creator, her Lord, the King "soon come".

She's quivering!
Can't you feel it?

An Admonition

Crumble, you marbled statue
Let your sands sift through an hourglass
Of a new day filled with
Changed attitudes, focuses and ideals

Soften, you hardened rock
Let your softness become pillows
Of new energized hopes and dreams
That many may rest their strategies upon

Melt, you frozen ice
Let tepid waters surround and warm the hearts
Of those cold from deep-seated anger
As they let go of negative thinking and hidden
fears

Humble yourself, you arrogant world
Let your humility improve the quality of life
For all - feed your hungry
Shelter your homeless
Love one another, while time there is still!

A Bucking Mule

I've never been on a bucking mule
I imagine it's kind of a rough ride
I've never been on a bucking mule
Straddled across its backside
But I've been on the backside
Of this old world
For quite some time now
Felt it bucking and jerking
Leaping and lurching
Trying to toss me off somehow
Recently though
It's gotten kind of slow
With a lurch here and there
But I'm holding on good and steady
I guess this old world
Has finally seen
I'll got off
When
HE's good and ready!

Divisive Spirit

There abounds a divisive spirit in this day
I know not from whence it comes
But its presence is strong and prevalent
Never have there been so many
Lips - moving, yet silent
Arms - welcoming, yet empty
Hearts – warm, yet cold
Doors – open, yet closed
Sisters, brothers, fathers, sons
Mothers, daughters, neighbors,
People...
We must recognize the factious spirit
It lacks gentleness and meekness
Its confluent with contentiousness
It is ugly
We must reject it and conquer it
We have but
A brief time here
to reconnect, to share, to talk
to love.

Still

When frills and ribbons and lace were few
Still, joy and laughter and love came through
When friends and pals and cronies turned away
Still, hope and trust and faith did stay
When rivals and strangers and foes were unkind
Still, joy and peace and love I did find
When moms and dads in life were spent
Still, a message of love He sent
Though ears of compassion and caring are few
Lo and behold, He sent me you!

Cold Back

Her back is cold
The coldness lingers
Enhanced by chilly silence
Of a cold lonely world
She longs for the warmth of yesteryear
Words of welcoming genuine ardor
Present words are frigid stings
Coupled with frosty breaths
Of gossipy polar bears
Piercing deeper her warmth-seeking flesh

The sun sets on a chilly winter's day
One thought is…soon it will be too late
With fading warmth of lost suns
She'll surely freeze overnight
As ice cycles form
Glistening in the failing sunlight…
And just as all hope is fading…
She hears a whisper… *no need to fear*…
Then, reaching deep inside
She realizes… my Lord – how faithful…
He provided for her a thermal jacket.

Soft Bottom Flats

She now wears quiet soft bottom flats
With gentle round toes
It makes better sense, really
She put those stiletto-heeled,
Square-toed stilts away
Way, way back in the closet
She goes quietly now
Not wanting to be noticed
Unlike back then
When like a dark chocolate candy bar
In a mixture of vanilla fudge
Went unnoticed
Then, she wanted to be noticed
Couldn't wait to get into those clip-clopping hills
Clip-clopping down hard paved roads
Catching an eye, turning a head
With Tina Turner legs… didn't know where she
was headed
Or why - just wanted to be noticed
One night she discovered that the turning heads
were square
And the catching eyes were piercingly cold.
Now as she dons her soft bottom flats
With gentle round toes

She quietly observes choices of round heads
And eyes that are gently clear.

Ear of the Soul

We must listen
With the ear of the soul
We must listen
In this time
Earthly ears cannot hear
Blocked by worldly debris
Worldly stuff
Cluttered canals
Only the soul's ear
Can hear
The daunting rush of the sea
Mother Earth's warning scream
Of the alarming warmth of her being
The silence of peace
The cries of the children
We must listen
With the ear of the soul.

The Good & The Bad of Man

I Watched You

I watched you
I studied you
I mimicked you
So I did as a child
I saw strength
I saw courage
I saw *Love*
Determination, Conviction – *Love*
No-nonsense Perseverance – *Love*
Confidence, Absoluteness – *Love*
Oh yes, I watched you
Looking beyond your outer cover
I saw the true essence of you
I saw *Love*
And so, today I mimic your strength, your
courage, your faith
The proud Nubian queen you were
Today, my mind's eye watches you still
A little red dress with pleats
The joy and magic of Christmas
Enhanced by your gifts of love –
A fruit cake, a handkerchief, a pair of socks…
Small gifts of love, yet so big as to remain in
joyful memories

Memories of family, love, happiness
The love we all shared
I have them with me forever
And so, I thank you, because now
I realize
"You watched us too!"

Grandeur

Hotel Grandeur - a four-star wonder
Found in the heart of Macau
Grandeur of the Seas - a cruise ship
Luxurious from stern to bow
The Dizzying Grandeur of Rococo
An 18th century art style
Accentuating aristocracy, yet
Shunning the meek and mild
Is grandeur a self-proclaimed sanction
For only the proud, the swank?
Or is it a quality born innately
Inclusive of the humble, the quaint?
Like the grandeur of a simple rose bud
The microscopic grandeur of life in a single drop
of blood
The grandeur of a babe's first word
The wondrous flight of a simple bird
The spectacular grandeur of a colorful forest
Arranged by hands of an October florist
or....
The grandeur of a gentle man's speech
That speaks loudly to the depth of his soul's
reach.

A Seedling

A seedling
Dispersed by a mother tree
Carried by winds
To a distant forest
Understanding this
Just a pause in its journey
It takes root
It grows

In the midst of other
Dispersed seedlings
It cultivates
In occasional taxing
Jungle

It expands
Vehemently protective
Of its own space
Yet, acknowledging
Appreciating
And counseling
The corners of others
Birch, oak, maple and the like

It spreads its limbs
With comical antidotes
Turning a sometimes puckish jungle
Into a mirthful
Lenient forest
Nourishing
All nature around it

Frogs bounce
From its limbs
Landing upside down
In the shade of its
Wind-blown leaves

Squirrels and rabbits
Prune from its wisdom
Hushing
Garrulous plumes of chatter

Yet, soon it uproots
Replants and reassigns
Obediently
Spreading its mirth
In seas of other
Taxing jungles.

Shift of an August Moon

Again she effortlessly appears
Against the backdrop
Of a shimmering dark canvas
She takes on the night shift
Mysteriously, glowingly
Relieving a jealous sun
A moon shift
Not as brilliant as her rival's
Not as glaring
Not as loud
Yet her uniqueness
Contrasted against a
Blackened sky
Stands out
And she effortlessly, stunningly
Works it
Teasingly showing only bits and pieces
Halves and quarters
Then on occasion,
A sudden flaunt of fullness
Her mystic beauty incomparable
Her shift ends
As the racket of the day shift enters
The sunny show-off

Sparkling colors everywhere
Hot, loud and boisterous;
The August moon then
Retreats - relaxed, peacefully, quietly
Until her next effortless appearance.

Tossing a Ball

The echo of waves' resounding clashes
To the mind's ear - recurring laughter

The sand teasingly tickles the skin
Swirling about by gentle force of the wind

Soft billowing clouds in the sky
Smile deeply as they float fleetingly by

The sun peeks out briefly in between
Acknowledging approval of this amorous scene

Even foliage on the arms of distant trees
Display joyful faces as they dance in the breeze

As the father tosses a ball to his son
I too marvel the interaction, the fun

Reaching for the ball, little fingers stretch out
Mimicking what dad has so patiently taught

Their effect on nature goes unseen
They, occupied only by each other's gleam

The innocent child, how blessed he is
A father, to share his joys, dispel life's fears

Staring across a vast blue sea
My mind ponders glaring scenes in the inner-city

Where so many little ones will never know
Absent fathers to whom they cannot go

Like my dad, as I reflect and sadly recall
Never tossed to me, a ball.

Schizoid

Encompassing one sinewy shell
Two faces in limited space dwell
They both peep from behind the same blind
Never before seen at the same time
The features, all one and the same
"Who are you now, the breeze of freeze's
name?"
Lexis emits from familiar palate
Recognizable only from time and habit
Flows like gentle summer breeze
Or like an erratic gale's winter freeze
Never sure just who loiters there
One minute a summer's gentle air
Whispering sweet melodious tunes
Causing a dampness where cranny blooms
The next minute gale-force winds
Whose crashing song causes sweet liquid's end
In the midst of ecstasy from summer breeze
Out of nowhere appears winter freeze
An icicle I snap from his side
And drives it between hard frozen eyes
Now, neither breeze nor freeze does bring
I suffocate in an airless spring.

I know how to wait

i know how to wait
like we had to wait
to sit on the bus
to sit where we
pleased on the bus
like we had to wait
for a crumb
of the pie
like many still wait
and barely get by
but at least
i know how
to wait

so I'll just wait
like we used to wait
for mamma
to get off the bus
with bag-filled goodies
cookies, popcorn and such
so we'd wait
 'cause we knew
she'd get off that bus
but at least

we learned how
to wait

like i hope one day
you will come
while i'm still home
before i'm gone
so, i'll just wait
'cause you see
i know how
to wait

and if you do come
after i'm gone
i'll leave you this poem
so you'll see
my spirit will be
here still… waiting
'cause it too
knows how
to wait.

Love

Baby

Love, romance, passion...
Deemed these guys a thing of the past
Knew them before, long ago
Reckoned I'd seen ultimate fireworks,
Savored yesterday's ecstasy of romance
The sun's setting in a cool yet colorful sky
Fires dying out
Then.... you.... now....
Your touch has re-awakened
Soulful sleeping volcanoes
Spewing years of built-up lava
Rekindled fires
Fueled like eons of dried brush
You stroked me to the edge of insanity
Sent the fireguards running, I did...
Discarded long-held house rules
As I no longer needed either
Unlocked me, you...
With keyed qualified idiom
Releasing captives through luscious reprieves
Opened locked doors
Receiving all that was really meant for you
Baby, you called me
A miracle potion that unblocked all arteries

To a passion-starved heart
I breathed you in, deeply
The sun is at high noon…
I am forever in love, my love.

Oh, A Tree

Oh, to become intertwined
In your mangled roots
That tie you firmly to earthly soil

Oh, to feel the texture
Of your debarked trunk
Against the smoothness of inner thighs

Oh, to savor the drippings
Of your sticky bittersweet sap
On arid lips

And, in the spring of time,
Oh, to hold each newly-blossomed twig
Against nurturing breasts

And, then
During a fall season
Oh, to mount the climax of your stature,
Sit upon your uppermost limbs
Experience ultimately
The epitome of all experiences -
To behold in exploding full-view -
One chromatic breathtaking masterpiece

A Cyberspace Encounter

Their orbits crossed
His flight suit attracted her
Hers attracted him
They sent digital signals
Soon to meet on earth
They met
Earth's atmospheric pressure
Revealed a different
Measure to each suit
From an earthly perspective
They both looked different
So covered up, unrevealing
He stripped his off
She stripped hers off
He obviously was pleased
She loved what she saw
His true form
Cover gone
Trusting, kind, giving
He couldn't decide
Keep the flight suit on
Keep it off
One minute it's on,
The next minute it's off

He couldn't seem to make
Any decisions on his own
So accustomed, he was, to clicking
On decision-making keys
So, again, he sought help
From twin search engines
They told him to put his flight suit back on
And continue flying
He did
He's back in orbit
She'll always remember him
With his flight suit off
Yet, she's enlightened from the experience
Content now to make earthly choices
With no need any longer
For orbits, flight suits and such.

A Moment in Time

Imagine
Having gone all day
Without eating
Then finding yourself
In an all-you-can-eat
Soul-food restaurant
Biting into the spiciness
Of a tender chicken leg
Cooked just like Aunt Bessie's.

Imagine
A sweet thirst-quenching
Tall glass of cold ice tea
On a 90-degree summer's day
Sweet liquids filling
To delightful ecstasy.

Imagine
An ice cream cone
Peaking at the top
One scoop of chocolate
One scoop of butter pecan
After a stressful day at work.

Imagine
An outfit
That flatters your form
Like the skin on a cobra
You keep it on
For the rest of your life.

Imagine
Outside
A warm summer's night
Lying flat on your back
Peering up at a clear starlit sky
Experiencing heavenly blissful peace
That only the presence of such majestic divinity
can allot.

All were mine one moment in time
I spent in the presence of a King.

Cultural

A Real-Man-Voice

Imagine, a voice
Speaking to a soul that longs for the hum
Of a real-man-voice
One rich with wisdom
From experiences of distant shores
Affluent with fortunes
From the heritage of African roots
Seasoned lightly with a hint
Of Cameroon's rich dark soil
Resonating a simile
Of cultural experiences
Disclosing facts of a life blessed
With happy seasons, challenged
By testing seasons, yet appreciative
Of knowledge gained from both
Imagine a voice
Vibrant with confidence of unfaltering faith
Booming with strength
From years of perseverance
Yet whispering gently
With underlying calmness
Like the serenity of a peaceful sunset
In the backdrop of a sleeping lake
A hum evidencing tunes of a real-man-voice

Whose source apparently
In synch with its world.

A Faraway Place

As I gaze deeply into your mahogany face
I see my home in a far-away place
The velvety darkness of your cover
Is not so different from that of my mother
As your fingers elegantly twist my hair,
I wonder of my fate had they not taken us from
there
As you expertly twist and braid each lock
The words you utter, I understand not
I wonder who would I be
If my ancestors were left there to be free
Perhaps we would have been friends
Perhaps we are even akin
Would I have your confidence, grace and proud
stance
Had I spent my life in my motherland?
I know there are problems from whence you
come
But none like being in a motherless home
And so my sister, when you're done with my hair
Don't be alarmed should I turn and stare
Into your dark and beautiful face
There, I see my home in a faraway place.

ME

The Outside Me

It used to be
When I'd look at me
Through the eyes of others

I was painfully aware
That what I saw there
Appeared not on magazine covers

Blond hair, skin fair,
Thin lips, slender hips,
This the favor of my brothers?

Warped vision of what beauty truly is
Unlearned lies throughout the years
I have now recovered!

Now I see
When I look at me
Through my eyes and not through others

I am reverently aware
Of what I see there
A replica of my Nubian mother

Smooth chocolate mahogany skin
Proudly displaying my African kin
Kinky twists adorn my hair
My lips full and voluptuously there
Not a single trace of silicone
This splendor is naturally born

What I see is innately sumptuous
My beauty is magnificently scrumptious!

Do you know me?

Do you know me?
Didn't we struggle in the same place
Shed tears over absent lace
Wasn't our pain intertwined
Your tears often blended with mine
Didn't we dream of a different life
A big house, loving husband, beautiful wife
Didn't our smiles hide hunger-frowns
As we adorned ancestral hand-me-downs
Didn't we witness life's conquered fears
Fought victoriously in the midst of mother's tears
Didn't we hail in the lap of this queen
Who taught, "*never forget from whence you come…*
Or what you've seen."

Didn't we struggle in the same place?
Drank life's water from the same vase
Overlooked lack of material pleasures
As mother's love brought unparalleled treasures
Wasn't our childhood bliss combined
As we drank of life's unblemished wine
And now, many years have passed
Some dreams brought to fruition at last

You, a big house, lovely children, a beautiful wife
And me, a long sought *"tranquil"* life.

So, despite the struggles and the pain
Please know that I am the same
The same gentle quiet demeanor
Enhanced by a wiser yet stronger tenure
So, when jealous foes who know nothing of me
Speak blatant untruths about me
Please, remember what you know of me…
For we struggled in the same place
Drank life's water from the same vase
Our pain intertwined
Your tears often blended with mine
We smiled to hide hunger-frowns
As we adorned ancestral hand-me-downs
Yet, mother's love brought unparalleled treasures
Despite often lack of material pleasures

Weren't we blessed with strong loving mothers?
Who taught: victory… is simply… loving one
another!
Do you know me?

Aging

Fifty

Do you remember back then
When frames were firm and thin

When sitting, nothing hung over a lap
Could wave an arm and see no flap

When a mind was quick as a whip
No fuzz above a then luscious lip

Yet, still, today we are blessed
Having withstood many of life's tests

Remembering precious little babies
Developed now into grown men and ladies

Staring into a revealing mirror
This life's journey has never been clearer

Through the joy, the pain, and the tears
Still looking good despite the years!

Though many valleys and mountains were
crossed
Here, this moment, we can say, nothing lost

Gladly, proudly and humbly we proclaim
Through Him, there's been only gain

We're here, in this time, today
Because He helped us find the way

What more could one ask for
So you're fifty! Look forward to fifty more!

Roller Coaster Ride

As we get older, shouldn't life get easier?
Like a roller coaster ride it often gets queasier
In youth, we survive any altercation
With a strong sense of determination
Alas, in the winter season of life
As problems stab at us like a knife
We grow angry, bitter and cold
Like an old wooden stove
Shattered, beaten, broken and bent
Whose ability to give off warmth is long spent
How did we get to this state?
How do we get rid of the bitterness and hate?
There is but one answer in this scene of the show
We must now "let it go"
And spend our last days on this earth
As if the giving of love is an unquenchable thirst
Place past hurtful events in the mind's archives
Of sealed, preserved impenetrable files
And make your roller coaster ride less queasy
As we get older, life should get easy.

Not Yet

Suspecting the tide's
Coming in soon
She contemplates
Her exit
Reluctantly…
For the dock is soothing
Despite ambushing bolas
Crawling about
Nibbling often at
Exposed brown
Rising frigid waters
Lap about the dock's surface
The pests are washed
Away…
Frigid waters
Recede
As she contemplates
Her stay
On the dock
A while longer.

Janice Beaty Springs was born March 8, 1950 in Winston-Salem, North Carolina. Janice earned a B.S. Degree in Business Administration from Trinity University in Washington, DC. She received an Editor's Choice Award in 2006 from the International Library of Poetry. Her work has been published in two anthologies: "A Surrender to the Moon" 2005; "A treasury of American Poetry" 2004.

Janice presently works in Alexandria, Virginia and lives in Bowie, Maryland. She is the proud mother of a beautiful daughter, Tyra.

Breinigsville, PA USA
28 September 2009
224871BV00001B/5/P